THE VULNERABLE TRUTHS OF AN ANXIOUS MIND

The Vulnerable Truths Of An Anxious Mind

LILIAN GRACE

Lilian Grace

Contents

First Printing, 2022

This book is dedicated to anyone in need of comfort in a dark time.
May you feel this book connect with your soul and leave you feeling understood.

And if you're struggling, remember to reach out to someone.

Thank you to everyone who took the time listened me.

Picking Up The Pieces

Would You Hate Me Too?

Choking on the fumes,
Hatred burning my eyes;
The gas gage
Climbing higher,
Hands steadying the wheel.
I see a child in the reflection,
Cheeks covered
In tear stains;
She waits,
But I drive away.

Headlights;
Squinting,
The lingering light
Away;
As a stunned deer,
My eyes sting
That loathing smell,
I have
For these yellowed beams.

Suffocation!
Jaw clenched,
Aching to cry out;
I am a lost echo,
Bouncing

Off the walls,
To find another voice;
Anyone.

A tangled mess
Of forced smiles,
Lungs exhausted;
My seatbelt,
holding in place
The last of my efforts.

If only love were as easy
As hating myself,
Maybe then,
I wouldn't be here;
As an ostrich,
My head buried,
Between the sands
Of my paranoia.
Struggling forward,
Nakedly self-aware;
What if they knew...

If I showed you my true self,
Would you hate me?

As a theatrical dance
My personas unfold;
Severe depression
Masking my innocence,
Anxiety
Faking her confidence,
While the exhaustion
Of running

From my own body,
Finally caught up with me.

The sign taunting, 80km/h.
Numb,
That's all I felt;
I've lost all sanity.
90...100...110...

I can't feel the steering wheel...

Bathroom Sink Pep Talks:

Staring blankly,
My own worst critique
In this small confinement
I stand over
The bathroom sink.

To draw smiles
On the fog of a window,
In hopes
Of brighter days.

The heavy sigh,
Emerging from my lips
As thick cream,
Poured,
Into the mug of
My depression.

Looking into
That murky mirror
Of my soul,
Wishing,
I could awake;
To feel the sticky calm
Roll across my tongue,
An aftertaste of joy.

The Self-Harm Of My Mental State:

My mind a greying quilt,
Devoid of colour and warmth;
As I lie on the floor,
Reaching for the doorknob.

This dizzying life
Splinting my thoughts,
Like a pod of peas,
Scattered along the realities of my indecision.

My brain screams like a freight train,
As I unravel this uneasy desire to hide.

Trapped in the bathroom,
Locked in
By my pigeon-like stupidity;
Always returning
To my home of anxious habits.

I need to get out of here.

Of A Dreamer's Self-Doubt:

I roll the film of my life
Across the floor;
Wondering if time,
In his crafty nature,
Had snipped it
To tuck some away.

Knelt on the ground,
Overwhelmed,
As a speck of dust
In the sand;
By the numerous
Empty spaces,
Yet to fill.

That creeping deadline,
Knocking over
An unfinished moment;
Just as I was beginning
To gain control again.

I watch it end,
Another year passed;
Drifting as a cloud,
Far away;
Before I could even

Say goodbye.

My frivolity
A fallen petal,
Broken,
From the slightest
Snap;
The harsh reality,
Of a sensible breeze.

A violent sorrow
Sliding,
Past the frame of my chin,
To caress
That sickening paranoia,
Lodged in the roots
Of my writer's block.

It drops
Along with my gut,
Ready to trip
My perfectionism;
Until there is nothing left
But a puddle
Of loathing tears.

I stumble,
Scratching out the letters
From my heart,
Replaced by those monotonized lines
Of tomorrow's next best seller;
A grovelling pause,
Hesitancy,
There my heart spills over again.

I feel as useless
As an eraser to a pen;
For I dream,
The vibrant romantic I am,
With hints of golden hope.

Flickering Doubt:

What of broken souls,
Whose flares are mistaken
For shooting stars;
While the lanterns they light
In your dreams,
Have yet to spark
Across your eyes.

Or have you forgotten their cries,
Pressing against,
As scissors
Cutting,
Through frail bones;
Reminding you
That you are not alone,
In the flickering doubt
Carved along your mind.

An Echoed Sorrow:

The rain sees me crying,
Whimpers softened by
Its peppering tones;
Scents of an autumn seasoning.

Lifting my chin,
It lets my tears roll
Down;
Sliding between the cackling laughter
Of the thunder,
Spilled on its clouded fingers.

I peer into the eyes
Of the storm,
Tasting its milky sorrows
As it sighs,
Finally,
Something as broken as me.

Afraid Of The Dark:

I often lay awake,
To see what lurks
Within the feared hours
Between my sleep.

Shadows look familiar,
Perhaps the demons
From my nightmares;
While my feet lay
Tucked away,
From the grasping hand
Beneath my bed.

If only I hadn't found
The strangers in my closet,
Then I might dream peacefully
Without these quiet prayers.

Anxiety Attacks:

And just like that,
I reach the place,
Of blacken clouds.
As a ship in the brewing waves,
I collapse,
Crying out in vain.

Butterflies
That once fluttered,
Overrun by moths;
Feasting on my last ounce of hope;
While I starve myself
In the name of irrationality.

Eyes,
Falling,
With each sharp gust,
As a leaf to fall unwillingly,
To the agony, I am submissive;
Failing to give
Even the slightest ode
To my standard lens of life.

Surges,
Sliding across my back,
As a serpent

Biting along the spine.

A lump seizing my throat,
Like the wind propels
A daunted sail,
Suffocating what's left of
My sanity.
Heaving chest aches
Motion me deeper,
Into the dizzying waves.

Shoulders,
Grasping at the ears,
Arching,
To comfort my soul;
A stiffening embrace,
Curling into
The inevitable time-bomb
Of suppressed panic.

Choking on words,
The guilt of compliance
Aiming at its target,
I feel it pierce my skin;
Pulling my hair,
As I press into my skull,
Attempting to free
My mind of this pressure.

The inaudible screams
Exhaled through shaken breaths,
Buried in my hands;
As the dead, I lay buried
In my agony,

Silent to the world.

Envying the tears
Falling freely from my paralyzed form
Wishing not to feel so utterly,
Hopelessly,

alone.

Affliction In Every Corner:

But life isn't easy
For anyone.
Like a sunset,
With colours all distinct;
To flip the pages of a book
One, unlike the other,
Our stories remain our own.

Left In The Dust:

Everyone else can go;
Pack up and leave,
No struggle.

No crying on the bathroom floor,
Sinking into myself,
Waiting for the next wave
To drag my body along the shore.

No plan B
In case they fall apart,
Or overthinking all the little things.

Because they can go,
Without looking back;
While I'm left behind
To catch up.

Blurred Consciousness:

It is only when I squint
Between the blurred lines,
Of open reality
And that secluded insanity
I place behind my eyelids;
Where I find myself calmed.

As the harsh edges
Of rationality
Are stripped away,
Allowing my crowded mind
To inhale the visionary images
Once opposed;
Emerging from their hiding;
Brought into submission
By the lucid dream,
That is to be still.

As anxiety continues,
Faltering on the lines
I've jumbled,
To cope;
It is here,
That the pain lingers,
Like a sledgehammer
Crushing my skull.

While my jeering shadow,
Creeps out,
From its mentally exhausting shell;
As fragile as a drop of dew,
Amidst the persona
That is
My masking smile.

Behind Closed Doors:

Everyone else can live
As though they fear nothing of this world,
Chins up,
Poised and smiling;
Their cup never spilling
Over the rim.

But everyone is broken
In one way or another,
We need only to peek
Behind closed doors
To see the glass shatter,
Or taste the poison
Spewed from cursing lips.

Happy? Birthday:

This day,
I hoped, would be different;
But I've done it again,
Once more.

Throwing optimism
Across the room;
As that one stone,
Forgetting to skip
Along the water,
I watch her drown,
Leaving her with my youth.

To be a giddy child
Just one last time,
We were
So confident then;
The world,
A freshly seasoned scallop,
To fit perfectly
Within our grasp.

Another day another dollar;
If only I had held on
To the pennies I spent,
Clutching,

Those fruity flavours
Scattered,
In that wafer-thin plastic.

I wish I could say I am better,
Though adulthood
Is never so kind;
With its screaming reminder
That another year
Has come and gone
Too fast.

This day,
I hoped, would be different;
But I've done it again,
Once more.

Spitting out
The promise of peace,
Letting it drop
Next to the candles;
Unwillingly placed
In a row,
As the ever-changing
Heights,
Marked in a door frame.

Today is my birthday.

You're Leaving–Right?

As a fire extinguisher
Behind the glass
Of my caution,
I remain prepared
To fight for my life,
Ready to lose you
At any moment.

Planted In Pain:

Lost,
In an unending void
Of quivering silence;
Hands in my hair,
A scream stuck to my lips,
I search for the gap
Between existence and death.

Nails on a chalkboard,
I wince within the ache of my soul;
Carrying what little hope I have
In this box full of holes.
If only I could escape myself.

For the leaves may come and go,
Drifting away
From the sting of winter,
But the tree remains;
However dead and hopeless,
Its roots cling to the soil
That taints my heart.

Apprehension:

The pressure on my mind
To spill out the words
I have yet to form,
Stuttering amid the headache
As this broken record plays
Scratching over
The sounds of my thoughts
Before they are even written.

Whose Side Am I On?

I wish I didn't relate
To villains,
In such a way;
As a candle waits
For the pitch of night,
We grow accustomed
To the shadows around us.

Knowing,
Those tortured scars
Of my sanity,
Left to wonder,
Why am I calmed
By their maniacal eyes?

Transfixed,
By the shards of glass
Piercing, through their gaze;
Collected from those
Invading scopes
Used to examine their flaws.
There, I see the truth
In the lies they were fed.

Here,
Where overthinking is glorified

In its new genius;
Murdering my thoughts
Into submission.
I call it relaxation,
Though really, it is simply delaying
The inevitable depression
That crawls up onto my bed
During the night.

After all,
Why waste my life,
As an hourglass
Flipped,
One too many times,
Going in the wrong direction;
When I could listen to everyone,
And strive for a success,
That was never mine.

They build my walls
Higher than I had designed,
As that itching desire,
The wood bug is eating away;
Ignores my human existence;
Focusing its energy
On killing my own identity.

Silence fuels my pain;
Words may strike like knives,
But I cut myself,
Deeper still in the quiet.
Because the cage by itself
Is not so frightening,
It is how you are lured

That haunts the mind.

So utterly intoxicated.
Emotion,
A bitter taste,
Just for you;
Until there is no other thought
But to go deeper.

But I've been there for a long time,
Just there, sitting in the cage;
Wondering, why they took me,
Why they kept me,
What I did wrong,
When the weight will go away...

For sometimes, it feels
As though sanity
Is more expensive,
Then letting my body
Stop altogether.

At least then
I wouldn't waste my efforts,
Spreading over
The cracks in my skin;
Trying to remember
How many pills it will take,
To return to the idolized form of
"Normal".

To Break Our House:

Running on borrowed energy,
I watch you drain
As I drink the last of your strength;
The house slips
From your hands,
To rebuild our foundation
Again.

Our buds dried out;
Raw realities
Chipping away,
At the distant memories
Of our flowered love.
Like a block of cedar
We cry,
Longing to return;
A tree to the forest.

Afraid to stay,
Greater still,
The regret of rushing away;
To find another in your arms
When I still want you.

Frosted love,
Scars these empty roads.

We fade,
Starving for an ounce of warmth;
To this worn song,
Now a raspy whisper.

Is it worth it?

Stuck Between Transitions:

Just because the sun shines,
Breaking,
Through the cracks
Of the cotton skies;
Coated,
In dusky coffee grinds,
Their vivid stains
Pouring over
The fluffed skeletons.
It does not mean,
That I am yet dried out;
From the bitter spray
That splashes out
The rippling deep.

As the salt licks,
What's left
Of the trickling syrup,
I watch it glimmer in the sun;
The smell of its
Sticky saccharine,
Gushing out
The rim of his mouth.
Smiling maniacally,
As a storm,
About to swallow a ship;

He leaves,
Taking my golden nectar
With him.

Yet,
I still stand drenched,
The raindrops
Nibbling,
At the numb
On my fingertips;
Enjoying
The familiar taste,
Of the ocean's fingerprints,
Left,
On my broken smile.

Still,
Sun's flames cannot save me,
From the storm
Inside myself;
Though the water is calm,
I am, all the same,
A violent mind.

My thoughts,
Kept screaming,
Those taunting rings;
Echoes of insanity
In my ears.
They beg
For another taste
Of my glimmering joy;
Its syrup,
Stuck,

Between the folds,
Failing to muffle
My disruptive voice.

Scrolling Through Faces:

My mind throws up,
Acidic flavours of doubt;
As I look
At the people I long to become,
But will never be.

To Force A Smile:

If only,
Holding up a smile
Were as easy,
As giving in
To that nameless torment
I bury.

Forcing smiles,
Some are easy;
As the tricking beam
You place
Across your lips
To greet an acquaintance.

But there is one
Not so simple,
A trembling frown
Turned up
At its rusted corners,
Before you mutter
"I'm fine."

Cycles of Time:

To find the time
To count the grains of sand
Along the beach,
Or discover all the hidden voices
In the wind.

But I am a song
Stuck on repeat,
Rushing around the clock;
As time whirls around
Like a washing machine,
Never quite catching my breath.

To Be Forgotten:

As a bag of chips,
Crinkled near the end,
Only to be thrown away;
We are a fleeting memory,
A footprint
To be washed by the rain.

Remember:

It's fine...I'm fine.
I'm doing well, remember?

I can't remember the last time
I genuinely smiled...
When did I last laugh?
Everything is blurry,
Like time
Has swallowed my soul,
Refusing to let my mind relax.

It's fine...I'm fine.
I'm doing well, remember?

Like a painting by Picasso
I've always hated those paintings...
But maybe that's because
Some part of me feels a little bit
Crazy and misshapen myself.

Sometimes,
When someone cries
I laugh.
How could it be,
That when I'm truly sad
I can't even muster up

The courage to cry.

It's fine...I'm fine.
I'm doing well, remember?

I watch the sunset, and it looks so pretty
But all I can think of
Is the darkness
That proceeds to bleed out
As night begins...

When was the last time
That I looked in the mirror
And saw beauty in myself?
Why am I unhappy?

It's fine...I'm fine.
I'm doing well, remember?

Why does the noise of society
Proceed to drown out our voices?
Why is it that
We're all dying inside,
While striving to fit
The superficial definition of perfect?

It's fine...I'm fine.
I'm doing well, remember?

Remember...

Why can't I remember?

Rome:

They say Rome wasn't built
In a day,
So clearly,
It would take some time
To fix it too.
But unlike Rome,
I cannot wait around
Year after year,
Waiting for someone
To come along
And paste my ruins
Back together.

Fallen Optimism:

There is one sorrow
Felt in the swaying of your knees,
As your body begins to fall;
Heavy as the tears
That sting these weary eyes,
Or the piercing sigh
To form on your lips.
It buries you low inside of yourself
Until all you can hear
Is the small voice
In the back of your head.

The Edge Of Hope:

The headache
Plays with my hair,
Until I forget how to think;
Erasing all the pleasant dreams
Tucked away
Beside my hope.

A Penny For Your Thoughts:

A penny for your thoughts
They say,
But if I gave you all of them,
Then your debt
Would be mine.

And that is when
You turn your back
Upon my burdens;
Quick as a switch,
You shift,
That stolen penny in hand,
You run.

Crumbling,
Under the musty stench of success;
Too concerned
With the weight
Of our world's gaze.

Because giving me
Anything
Means nothing to you;
So why waste your time
Listening to my cries,
When you could simply forget

You ever knew me.

Why bother,
With the raging storm
Engulfing my eyes,
From which I beg you
To relieve.

Or those downward spirals
Chasing my thoughts,
Around the loops of my mind;
When you could gain my life
Instead,
And run away with it too.

Behind The Screen:

To scroll along
The sea of faces,
Countless
As the needles
Falling off a fresh pine;
I feel the need
To sweep up
Every last one.

Though eventually
I am consumed,
By that sinking guilt
Lying behind my eyes;
Pushing tears
Towards my cheeks,
Until I give in.

Obsessive
As a mockingbird,
To find a different voice;
I am reminded
I have failed to live up
To the expectations
Of those compulsive clicks,
The social demand
That I am no more

Than what can be seen
From a screen.

Regret:

I circle back,
As a dog chasing its tail,
To the old habits
Yet to die.

When suddenly,
I slip through
The salt of the Earth,
To find myself
In a coffin of unfinished dreams.

Strength In The Chaos

Green:

If only I could go outside;
And erase the corpses
Left by wilted leaves,
Until I felt the sun
Sinking into my veins again.

I'd coax the ivy
To rise along my legs,
So that I may forget, I ever knew,
The winds that once uprooted me.

To fill my body with green,
Covering my scars
With budding flowers;
Until the dead hands that grab me
Might wither away.

Don't Give Up Just Yet:

I hope you know
I found the rainbow
Sewn on to your back;
Proof that you were trying
All along,
To fight the haze that kept you
From seeing the rest of the world.

I smell the snap of fresh ginger
Masking your bitter tears,
Reminding those around you
You're still here;
Even when you wish
It were just a dream.

You hide the scars
Along your arms,
From the words
That broke your skin;
But you have come too far,
To let the rain
Drown you out.

Just because your tears
Can hide
During the downpour,

Does not mean
You'll never be noticed.
I see you...so don't give up just yet.

I Survived:

I survived this year.

The collage of my life,
An empty balloon
Devoid of interest.

A tattered heart
Broken glass,
To pick the shards up
Off the floor.

Silky memories
Veiled over smiling faces,
Of which I attempted to borrow.

But I survived this year
And maybe that is enough.

You Will Find Yourself Again:

Drowning in the deep,
Falling seams
An endless cry;
But the journey continues,
As these lows teach you
To come back to yourself.

Validation Is A Mortal Spotlight:

Human affection,
An ever-moving spotlight;
Drifting in search,
For the next ebb and flow
Of societal gossip.

Whisks of dread ensue,
As panic stirs the storm.
An unease,
Washed,
In the vanilla taste of the vague;
It settles,
Amid the hissing waves.
We tread frantically,
Attempting to find our name,
Within the surface
Of the salted ripples;
Grasping
At anything, anything at all...

Popularity,
As smoothened cedar,
Adrift,
Amidst the bellowing calls
Of the sea.
We seize it mercilessly,

Immersed in the smoky aroma;
Our damp soul,
Clinging,
Along the raft of security
That is our Earthly audience.

Though pleasure
Is only temporary,
As the world
Demands to be fed;
The tropical lies
We attempt to portray.
Its beam carries on,
To new trends
And prettier faces;
As glittering gold,
Only gathered to spend.

The lighthouse,
A raging war;
Forged,
On the backs
Of the jagged rocks.
Whose incessant envy,
Lies within the bitter taste,
Of the cunning tide.
While arrogance stays
A hidden pebble,
Buried in the sand;
Overlooked,
For the heavy stone, it is.

This system remains,
A masked sense

Of misplaced justice;
As rampant waters
Still shake the shores.
The mermaids,
Drowning us,
Ever so gently;
That no one should notice
Our screams,
Amidst their angelic lulls.

But when the rays of light
Do flicker away,
Our nerves begin to quake;
As we are trained,
To fix the inevitable truth.
The weed plucked,
As a tang of dandelions
From the soil;
We hope to remove,
The soured stain
Of our vulnerability.

We are told to be the light,
To the shadows in this world;
But as a candle glints,
In the twilight of a room,
We see only ourselves.
Yet, without a light upon ourselves,
We believe,
More often than not,
That we are nothing.
But maybe,
If our pride falls,
We might sink

To the ocean floor;
And remember
The dead soul beneath us.

While we chase after the spotlight,
As the moon can not
Catch the sun,
Our lives fail to capture
The ever-shifting eyes of society.
Only to recall our humility,
Pointing us back to the glory and light
That is God.

There Is Beauty Still in the Misery:

There must be a place for me,
A place for wandering souls.
How else would I carry on
Weary and battered;
Holding tight to the balloon
In my hand,
Lest my hope float away.

To return to happier times,
Where the colours of my youth,
Lay stamped on my cheeks;
Now drooping down
With the inky stain of my tears.

But this is one moment
In a lifetime,
Of a million memories
Yet to be;
So why waste
This passionate misery,
When I could use it
To paint a rainbow instead.

Words Hold Silent Wounds:

What are words,
But echoes of lost thoughts;
Drowned rats,
Taken too soon.
But we were mice,
Before intruded,
Through the eyes
Of the white knight;
Flaws succeed,
As focus shifts
To the dirty forager
Within humanity.
They spit against
The foulness,
Of our sin-stained tails;
Helpless,
A final taste of life,
Slipping from our tongues.
The smell of their clasped hands,
Joined in union,
Pulling us low;
We sink,
Beneath the harsh noises,
Until we are silenced.
Freedom of speech,
The blank slate coveted

By our dying individuality.
We believe the cloyed lies,
Trapping us;
As a circle,
Forcibly crammed,
Into the sharp edges of a box.

Though perhaps,
Were caution used,
A little wiser still;
Self-esteem might yet return,
Though swept,
As a rug pulled from my feet.
I stumble,
Falling,
Onto the vast stretch;
The floorboards
Of my ridged insecurities.
Motionless.
Paralyzed by the quicksand,
Of your so-called
"Constructive criticism";
Guilted,
By the shrill voice,
Of your sergeant tone;
Scented in scrutiny,
Laced with empty prayers,
Lingering on your breath.
Maggots,
Biting the bland shreds of strength;
Lost,
Amid fallen balance.

Pleading,

Of anyone,
To snip the strings,
Binding me to the contract,
That is a puppet's dance.
Am I not ill enough?
That mental health remains,
A stolen manipulation,
Of a marionette
Once controlled.
Even still,
The world proceeds
To flounder our success.
Though the theatrics must continue,
Whirling through
Charcoal-covered nights,
Lest we break.
But if we do,
Why must our confidence be stripped;
If we are unable to perform
While these puppeteers
Entangle the wires,
Only to curse our defective limbs.

Though if God took me away,
So that I might be understood,
He could take my hope,
Now held,
With a fragment of
Its formerly poised posture;
Where I left it,
At the bottom of the stairs.
Lifting my stale bones,
Off the ground;
The salted aftertaste,

Tainting my youthful flavours.
He would dust away the soot
From my mousy physique,
So that I could feel
The purity of his hands.
Unravelling all the strings,
Unbothered
By my creaking frame.
Resting,
The scrapped piece
Of my puzzle,
Among the body of brothers;
A home,
I forgot I had known.

But the painter only sees,
What he meant to create.
You justify
The bold colours of your opinions,
The paintbrush in your hand
Shakes,
At your wild motions.
It splatters,
Along my hands,
Pigments,
Grazing into the skin;
As your words hold silent wounds,
Etched into my mind.

Something must have broken,
Though notice,
You never did.
That God *had* taken me away,
Caressing my soul;

As a lovely peach,
The fruit of his eyes.
He washes off the tints,
That stain your remarks
Into my ears;
As I taste my confidence again.
He placed me in his palm,
Undisturbed
By what I was;
He sniffed the succulent juices
Of my being
And smiled.

To Paint With The Colors In The Back Of My Mind:

Pitch black,
Drawing out the voices
Harsh whispers,
Tempting the canvas.

Ignoring their calls,
Dipping the soft bristles;
Hope submerged
In blue-tinted tides,
That calms these roaring waves.

If only I could taste the sky again,
A bite of mango,
Juices dripping down my chin;
Or kiss the crackling flame,
As it caresses my skin.

I take the roses from my eyes,
For a moment
All is a blurred grey;
To be washed away
By the white of snow.
It falls along sprawling leaves,
Until the green
Comes back once more.

And so, I paint a rainbow
Amid these bleak clouds;
Finding my way back,
For innocence knows nothing
But colour and light.

The Way Back To Myself:

As a child sent
To the corner down the hall,
Watching the wall
More so than my tongue;
I learned the hard way.

Screaming
Over the shutting door;
Masked confidence
To fade
With the embers
Of our dysfunction.

A jungle
That is the world;
For it is only
In the chaotic wilderness
Of our relationship,
Where I learn
To fall back on myself.

The Art Of Precaution:

I wish my troubles fell
From the sky
Like a gentle rain,
But perhaps, it is better
As a harsh wind;
So one learns to take an umbrella
Before they face a storm.

Just Breathe:

Relax.
Picture an ocean.

Inhale.

But the rocks cut my feet.
Waves crashing,
Surrounding my sanity;
I'm drowning.

Exhale.

Find a safe place.

Inhale.

I feel arms around me,
Hugging my soul;
Peace,
Blanketing over this restless body.

Exhale.

I feel everything stop.
I can just breathe.

Finding My Way Back To Faith:

Stuck listening to the silence,
Waiting on your voice again;
Feeling nothing but my pity
Seeping through my wandering prayers.

I wish I could say
We've grown closer,
But lately, you're farther away;
Or is it me?

I've done everything you've asked;
I tied myself to your name,
I tried to live for your love,
But you left me to fall.

Or did I forget?
That you're still here,
Even when the body breaks,
Reminding me of your heart.

I reach towards
Your outstretched arms,
To feel you embrace
The holes in my soul;
Until all that I am
Is filled with your mercy.

My body is wiped
With the white dove
Of your robe;
As I live to love you once more.

Erasing You From My Memory:

The hardest part of our goodbye
Wasn't in walking away;
It came after.
On the days
I lay,
Crying myself to sleep,
Pretending you never existed.

But now that you've drifted away,
Along the river of my tears;
I can see my life
Free from the smudges of your lies,
As I erase you from my memory.

Holding On:

My arms stretched
As a plant waiting to grasp the sun,
Sitting still in anxious silence.
I drift past yesterday's flaws,
Into the spirals
Of today's scattered agenda;
Trying my best
To fill the cracks in my days
With the colours of tomorrow's hope.

To Find the Light Above the Clouds:

Pushing through the grey,
I break the clouds;
Parting as a swept curtain,
Against the winds of change.

I feel the sun
On my cold skin,
Devoid of light for too long;
I bask in the rays
Of this gentle reminder,
It will get better.

Stretching the Boundaries Between Words:

Words,
A shifty construct;
To be as calm
As a drop of honey
On the tongue,
Or as deadly
As the dagger
Shot from an eye.

They could change the world
If we let them;
To challenge
The system,
And become as free
As the innocent eyes
Of a child.

Where the voiceless
Reach out in rebellion,
To stretch
The boundaries
Between words.

Their simple structure,
Expanded,
Along invisible lines

Separating the sky
From the Earth's veins;
To be the brighter version
They were meant for.

They stand,
Against a society
That deems
Silence is etiquette;
As superficiality
Becomes the new trend.

For a word itself
Is not so evil,
As the heart
Behind the voice.

Falling Back To Strength:

A bird may fall
Against a window,
Knowing not
What caused it to stumble;
Even still,
It gets up to fly again.

Of Unknown Journeys:

Sometimes,
We must stumble
On the pebbles
Found in the dirt,
To prepare
For the mountains ahead.

God The Creator:

I drew a line in the sand
To set us apart,
But the world's waves washed it out;
As it pushed me
Until I broke.

But you don't mind
My shattered pieces,
You pick me up off the floor;
To place them in a new order,
Reminding me to change
Into something new.

Progress:

To feel the sigh
Of my soul in your arms
Reminding me
Of where we've been;
Knowing
We have found a way before,
And will do it once more,
Again.

Healing:

One day,
He won't hurt you anymore.
One day,
You will think of him,
Seeing the distant memory of his face,
And smile again.

Perseverance:

As a bird chirps
Even in the chill of snow,
So I will sing
In the depths of my anguish.

Resilience:

I know now
How strong you must be,
To find your footing
In the rain;
Or swim against the current,
Even though your arms
Are all worn out.

Take Me Away

The Dawning Of Spring:

The pitter-patter of feathered songs
Brush along the ears
Of the early morning,
As robins scurry across the lawns
Of unsuspecting neighbours.

Crocus boasts
To be the first
Among the flowers
To touch the crisp air;
She spreads her petals proudly
So the children might admire her.

And notice the pussy willow,
Stretching out his limbs to yawn,
Whispering in a groggy voice
For its leaves to wake.

Or the little girl,
Whose giggles lie
Perched on the swing
Under a cherry tree;
To watch the dawning of spring.

Treelines:

Clouds,
Melting on her tongue;
She chased the trees,
Until she learned
To walk along the sky.

To Be Placed In A Meadow:

Strands of grass
Stretching out,
To touch
These wandering feet;
Wildflowers tickle my fingers
As I lay my body along the Earth.

The journey,
A bit longer than expected,
My bones moan into rest,
As all that I am
Is finally still;
I lie and watch the clouds.

Strawberries and Cream:

Her soul a fresh strawberry,
Bright and rosy,
Dipped in silky cream.
She stands,
Giggles and sticky lips;
Offering her heart,
To the boy
With the wooden spoon.

A Cabin In the Middle of Nowhere:

Take me to the mountains,
Show me a little cabin in the woods
Just for us.

The birds
Can be our alarm clock,
While the breeze
Carries us through the day;
We'll dance with the moon
Until the wolves sing us a lullaby.

Take me to the middle of nowhere,
Where no one will find us,
And we can simply live
To love life.

The Locker Room:

I enter quietly, as I often do.
The room abuzz
With the commotion
Of unsettled bodies;
Pieces of paper,
Stapled together
By the envelope of our towels.

Standing alone,
Pressed into a corner,
Praying,
I go unnoticed;
Though wincing,
Amid the hissing blares
Of my glowing embarrassment.
I glance around,
Before removing,
The blanket of security,
Hugging my silhouette;
Replaced by awkward shivers,
Concerning,
Such a public display of oneself.

Weighed down,
As waves of insecurities collide;
Lapping,

One over the other.
Nakedly apprehensive,
Towards,
The eye of the storm
Of silent judgement,
Passing between one another.
Analyzing the size
Of our bosoms and bottoms,
Always comparing,
In a vicious cycle
Of female drama.

Later we will return,
To groom out the flavour
Of our grass-stained bodies.
Attempting,
As a sandcastle resisting the tide,
To defeat any flaws
We may have acquired;
Over the past,
Strenuous hours
Of heat and exhaustion.

The must of sweat lingers,
As gym shorts and damp shirts
Are thrown to the ground;
Replaced by the elegance
Of humane garments.
Jeans and graphic tees,
When settled across our skin;
As if reawakening us,
To our normal, gossiping state.
Paired with the sweet fragrance
Of deodorant,

Reminding us
Of what we were
Before we entered this place.

Still You:

Searching for a new dress,
To find herself
In another persona,
Only to realize
The wardrobe she wore
Was lesser still
To her own smile.

From Midnight Into Morning:

I looked up,
Towards the ink-splattered sky;
It was calm and still,
And I realized;
The beauty in the darkness.

And so I stood there lingering;
Although,
It was important to note,
That sleep
Was stretching out his arm,
In attempts
To lure me back to bed.

But I stayed,
Captivated,
By the flicker of the moon
Behind
The scattered clouds.

The humming tranquillity
Of the silence,
Brought about
A certain accent,
To the noises
Of the early birds.

Lulled,
By the music,
As the stringed chords
Of the telephone wire
Join the orchestra
Of rumbling cars and stray cats.

Eyes filled with wonder,
As I concluded
That some moments
Were meant to be savoured.

A Home Is Meant To Be Lived In:

There is no picket fence
In my dreams,
No chandeliers made of glass;
But a little house
On a quiet road,
Where our memories can grow
Until they burst open
The colours of our love.

Sweet Tooth:

A Chicklet of a tooth,
That toying nuisance
Pulling violently,
At the bell in my stomach.

With the lust
Of a hundred men;
Failure to control
That growing urge,
Rubbing against
My bland tongue,
Ever to be satisfied.

If only my eyes
Were smaller
Than the freshly baked
Gluttony
Of my appetite.

Then perhaps,
I wouldn't find myself
Searching
A midnight pantry,
In order to fix
Your flirtatious cravings.

A Summer Trance:

Golden laughter ripples across
These lapping tides,
Nostalgia slips onto the tongue
Like soft ice cream;
To play in the grass again,
Unaware of time itself,
Falling into the bliss
Of a sunny afternoon.

Define Poet:

Poets are just children
Who never stopped
Dreaming.

She Who Made Me:

She held my life
In her gentle arms;
The joyful unknown
Of endless possibilities.

Carrying the scars
That she bore to bring me here,
These lines that furrow her brows
From the days
She helped me carry my sorrows.

She holds the patience
I wish I could grasp,
Seeing the good in everyone,
Never letting the lemoned days
Turn her smile sour.

She taught me what it is to be a woman;
To hold my head up high,
Remembering my worth
And what it means to love myself.

She did the best
With what she was given,
To make sure I knew
That I am loved;

Even if I didn't realize
Just how much.

Moving Forward:

Moving away
Is simply another journey,
Taken
Not to end your identity,
But to find yourself in a different city.

Images:

Pitter patters
Of the rain,
Chattering,
Among peppermint whispers
Of the wind;
Breathing
Through the trees.
Playing,
With the blades of grass;
Sliding down,
The twirling cracks
Of their spines.
A glossed taste,
Dashes of Chamomile,
Left to dissolve
Along the splashes
Of their dewy tongues.

Little pebbles,
Resting,
In the corner,
To watch the world;
With tiny legs,
All etched in dust,
Too stubbed to hold themselves up.
Observing hidden secrets,

With glimpses sharp,
For stones so smooth;
Possessing keener eyes,
Than even the dirt.
Waving greetings,
Heard by smiling tulips,
Glazed, with enamoured marks;
Traces of gentlemen,
Dipped,
In a honeycombed embrace,
To be a possession
Of the mischievous daffodils.

Blossoms yawn,
With rosy cheeked petals
Stretching past the boundaries of winter.
Blushing,
Their opening eyes,
Blinking sleepily;
At the fluttering rays,
Sun leaves behind
In her sleep.
Giggling,
Tickles of butterfly kisses,
Placed along the fingers
Of their stout,
Budding leaves.
Leaving them wanting more,
The sweet sniffles,
Those delicate wings;
A blanket of ocean waves,
Simple perfume,
Covered in the salt of the Earth.

Moments
Of unattainable beauty,
Captured,
In silent stillness;
Photographed,
Through the eyes of a window.

Life All Mine:

As the hush of
A hummingbird;
The locket around my heart
Clutching to
The hopes of tomorrow.

My heart, a little lighter,
While I focus;
Remembering only the warmth.

Sun-kissed flowers,
A lavender high surrounds me,
As I taste the smoky colours
Of gradual success;
A life that was and is
All mine.

Inspiration:

A tightened grip
To hold it still;
Pinned down,
Somewhere
Between my mouth
And these ink-stained hands.
That I might pluck the words
From this scattered thought,
Before it breaks free.

Simple Comforts:

Peppermint tea,
Sweet tangs
Of smoky delight;
Running along
The outlines of my smile.

Fond memories,
Relief;
As the sinking feeling
You taste just before
Falling asleep.

Whispers,
From the rain;
A rainbow is brewing;
Reminders,
Of my favourite moments.

Drifting Into Nowhere I Know:

I fell asleep
Beneath a floating cloud,
That drifted aimlessly
Towards a town
I had never been.

I awaken with a sudden stir,
Climbing down the ladder
Back to Earth;
To find my place
Among the foreign sands.

Nolan:

He was, as people say,
A mystery of a person.
Opposing all forms
Of stereotypical behaviour,
Shown by those
Of teenage minds.

While of talented hands,
He kept in the shadows
Of the avoidant and introverted artists.
Among the lost souls,
Immersed in passion,
He fit the daydreams
Of a fame-crazed citizen;
With a zest of enthusiasm,
Trailing behind his caricature.

Sunshine on his clothes,
The flair of a crisp auburn chapeau,
Unfolding the quirks,
He tries so hard to hide.
But none can bury
The spark of theatrics in his eyes,
Along with its ever-present lust
For applause.

These colourful soldiers,
Lead the rebellion
Against societal norms;
While waging war,
Over the human need for validation.

Butterflies:

Giving colour to the wind;
Rainbows gliding between the Earth,
Little imprints of joy
Perched on a leaf
A kiss with every footprint.

Of Autumn Atmosphere:

A quiet little café
On the corner of the road,
Where tea is poured
In smooth round mugs.

Fresh pastries melt,
Like honey on the tongue;
While egg runs down
The fork
In my left hand.

There sits a girl,
In a hazel sweater
With its sleeves wrapped
Over her palms;
Hoping to find a home
Among the bustlings
Of a crisp fall morning.

My Life In Movie Scenes:

I find the gentleman
In my mind,
Full of colourful wit;
Holding me in his arms,
Protection,
With an air of composure.

His words refresh my soul,
Their gentle ripples
Catch my breath,
My body eases at his touch;
He smells of home.

He carries me away,
Into the finesse
Of the Hollywood skies;
Dancing amidst
The spotlight of the moon,
Where we learn to shine like stars.

Within Reach:

The quiet of a whisper
Met me in a dream.
Leaving its lips parted
So I might look inside;
And see the joy
I had been searching for,
Was there within my grasp.

To Ease My Soul:

Freedom
Is the quiet urge
To do nothing but exist
As you are.

Bonfire Melodies:

His eyes danced with the flames,
Guitar in tune with the night;
Until finally
His heart flew away
Amid the soaring embers.

Fairytale Moments:

Blurred fantasies
Dance among
My scattered daydreams...

The feeling of flying,
The hope of reaching a life
Beyond your wildest dreams.
A place where dragons
Soar along the horizons,
Or fairies dance
In the spring;
A moment of whimsy
So indescribable,
One might wish it would never stop.

Today I Am Sick:

My reflection
A ball of yarn,
Chased profusely
By the pawing cat;
I stand careless today.

Baggy sweatpants,
Eyes worn from the light of day,
In a dimly lit room
I dream of a place,
Beyond this cell;
Reaching past the spell
Of raspy whispers and worn lungs,
That I lay confined to.

Today Is Good:

There is a place for you,
Where the willow trees
Brush along your hair,
While rays of summer sun
Caress your smile.

Here, the flowers envy your legs,
For you can walk away;
So enjoy today,
Stuff it in your pocket,
Don't let it slip away.
Because today is good,
And tomorrow may never come.

Lost In a Book:

Finding that soft space,
A warm pastry
To my scattered mind;
Reminding me to forget.

Lost within the ink of a book,
To flip between the pages,
Hearing them flutter;
As the delicate wings of a hummingbird.

I reach the place
Where no one can hurt me,
In a world away from all that I am;

About The Author

Lilian Grace is a small-town poet from Vancouver Island, who uses her writing skills to voice her inner thoughts.

She expresses her emotions to inspire others and strives to create a "safe space" for her readers to share their experiences with their own mental health struggles.

Get Connected

If you'd like to see more, come check out my pages!

Find me on:

Facebook (Lilian Grace)

Instagram (lilian_of_the_valley)

CPSIA information can be obtained
at www.ICGtesting.com
Printed in the USA
LVHW080103260123
737950LV00016B/1447

9 781738 832828